THE ART OF
ARABIC COFFEE

THE ART OF ARABIC COFFEE

Medina Ilyas

Medina Publishing

First published in 2023 by Medina Publishing Ltd
50 High Street
Cowes
Isle of Wight
PO31 7RR

www.medinapublishing.com

Copyright © Medina Ilyas, 2023

Printed and bound in the UAE by Oriental Press

ISBN (Paperback): 978-1-911487-78-4
ISBN (eBook): 978-1-911487-79-1

Medina Ilyas asserts her moral right to be identified as the author of
this book.

CIP data: A catalogue record for this book is available at the British Library.

Concept, text, and recipes authored by Medina Ilyas
Contributing editor: John Leonida
Recipe contributors: John Leonida, Sara Alali, Nooran Albannay and Fatma
Al-Baiti
Editor: Eugenia Petoukhov
Illustrator: Olha Rybtsova
Design and layout: Dragan Bilic & Alexandra Lawson

Contents

Foreword

I am both proud and honored to author the foreword for Medina Ilyas' book, *The Art of Arabic Coffee*, written to deliver the rich and vibrant Arabic coffee experience to coffee lovers worldwide.

Medina is one of the most inspiring women I have met in the coffee industry, and I admire her for her dedication, kind heart, leadership skills and positive approach to life. I was fortunate enough to meet Medina early in my career, shortly before accepting the challenge to compete in the Cezve/Ibrik Championship. During this time, it became my mission to reintroduce to the world one of the oldest methods of brewing coffee and showcase how we apply quality standards to this unique beverage and its preparation.

While getting to know Medina, I discovered that we share the same vision. We both strongly believe that it is essential to create more content about Arabic coffee and its unique brewing methods to make it more accessible to people who have never tried it before. Later, I was thrilled to learn she was writing a new book on the subject, and I am truly grateful to her for this important initiative. With her cross-cultural vision and multidisciplinary curiosity, Medina is your perfect guide to Arabic coffee.

Complete with a concise history of Arabic coffee, as well as the special serving rituals and spirit of hospitality that defines it, *The Art of Arabic Coffee* will take you on a journey of the unforgettable flavors and rich culture surrounding this quintessential Arab beverage. In addition, you will learn about the tools used to brew and serve your own Arabic coffee and how this beverage is unique in its brewing method and roasting style. Finally, this book will walk you through brewing your own coffee, step-by-step, and show you how to pair it with different spices to create delicious drinks with easy-to-follow recipes. So, read on and get ready to delight your senses!

Sara Alali
Founder and Co-Owner - THAT Boutique Cafe in Riyadh, Saudi Arabia
Barista trainer and Q-grader
Sensory judge in Qahwa Championship 2019
Host of The MAP IT FORWARD Middle East Podcast
World Cezve/Ibrik Championship Finalist

When I drink coffee with you, I feel that the first coffee tree was planted for us.

- Nizar Qabbani

عندما أشربُ القهوةَ معك أشعرُ أنَّ شجرةَ البنِّ الأولَى زُرِعتْ من أجلِنا.

– نزار قباني

Introduction

Hello! My name is Medina Ilyas, and 15 years ago I fell in love.

This wasn't the gentle, courtly type of love that starts with a giggle and ends with "till death do us part." It was a love of such great revelation that everything I thought I knew suddenly came undone. Let me tell you about it. I was visiting Oman for the first time when I was introduced to authentic Arabic coffee, or *qahwa* (pronounced *kah-wah* or *gah-wa*). It was true love at first sip! The taste left me both befuddled and mesmerized. I was intrigued by the ceremony, the culture and the artistry that went into making such a perfectly crafted cup of coffee. It felt like opening a secret portal into a rich new world. Since then, I have been lucky enough to discover and document hundreds of different recipes.

It took me 15 years to collect these recipes from across the Arab region and to conduct the research that has given me such an in-depth understanding of the rituals and traditions involved. Learning the skills to create my own variations of Arabic coffee has been a journey of discovery into a hitherto hidden coffee wonderland, and I am thrilled to be able to share this knowledge with you!

There is no better way to introduce Arabian culture and hospitality than by telling the story of Arabic coffee. As part of this custom, you will discover beauty, tradition, unrivalled coffee recipes and, most importantly, warmhearted people.

The Arabic coffee ceremony is much more than simply serving coffee. It is a ritual that involves connecting with friends, family and the community, as well as honoring one another by taking time to get together to share stories, a delicious drink and a warm experience.

Drinking Arabic coffee is more than a means to pass the time or refuel; it's an enriching cultural experience.

The intangible cultural heritage of Arabic coffee is hidden in the oral traditions that pass the recipes down from generation to generation. It is a goal of this book to document this heritage, and also, dear reader, to offer insights into the world of Arabic coffee in all its glory. So, please enjoy these recipes—try them out with your family and friends and use them as a valuable opportunity to connect with your tribe face-to-face, away from the distraction and the clamor of day-to-day life. Experience the unique character of Arabic coffee in the same way I did all those years ago!

This book will help you start your lifelong journey, enjoying this quintessential Arab cultural tradition. It will offer you a brief history of Arabic coffee, essential knowledge about the ingredients and their health benefits, a description of the ritual and fantastic recipe ideas. Whether you want to understand more about Arab culture, learn to make healthier coffee, slow down and be more mindful or simply try new recipes, introducing Arabic coffee to your life has the power to transform it for the better.

For me, Arabic coffee represents a secret passage to the mysterious culture of the Arab world. It is the silent language of hospitality for each family, each tribe, and each country. There are thousands of incredible recipes closely intertwined with family stories and traditions, and personally, I believe that if you want to discover, explore and understand Arabian culture, Arabic coffee offers a perfect way in.

*Wars have been planned over coffee, and wars have
ended over cups of it.*

- Arabic proverb

خُطِّطَ للحروب أثناء احتساء القهوة، وانتهت الحروب خلال احتساء القهوة.

– قول شعبي

1. The History of Arabic Coffee

Let's be honest, when most people think of coffee, they think of American coffee, French café-au-lait, Italian cappuccino or espresso, or—say it quietly—instant coffee. For many, coffee only exists in tall, grande or venti cups somewhere in the 32,000 branches of a company headquartered in Seattle or its many imitators. While many coffee lovers are aware that some of the best coffee beans come from Colombia, Jamaica and Costa Rica, what they may not know is that Yemen is the country where coffee has the most profound historical connection. Similarly, people may not associate coffee with Ethiopia, and yet it is where the coffee tree first blossomed. There is more to coffee than meets the eye—or the taste buds—and we routinely overlook the origins of this classic drink, which are overshadowed by mainstream consumerism and pop culture. So, let's take a step back and discover the roots of the humble arabica bean—the most famous coffee bean of all.

Arabica vs. Robusta Beans: What You Need to Know

While there are dozens of types of coffee bean, arabica (*Coffea arabica*) and robusta (*Coffea canephora*) are the two most common. The main differences between these two pertain to their taste, shape, strength, cost, geographical location and growth conditions, as well as their cultivation and harvest techniques.

Arabica beans typically have a milder, sweeter taste with slightly fruity undertones, while robusta beans have a more substantial, bitter taste with grainy undertones. They are also different in color and shape—arabica beans are dark green, flat, and elongated, while robusta beans are a lighter shade of green and have a round shape.

While arabica beans are the predominant bean type cultivated around the world, robusta beans contain more caffeine and are used primarily in instant coffee and as a filler in ground coffee blends. Arabica beans are more expensive than robusta and require more labor to cultivate, since they need to be grown at higher altitudes. Finally, robusta beans are principally cultivated in Africa and Indonesia.

Ethiopian and Arab Origins

Ethiopia is home to some of the oldest coffee-drinking traditions in the world, as well as the birthplace of *Coffea arabica*, the coffee plant. According to legend, one day, an Ethiopian goat herder named Kaldi noticed his animals became agitated after eating the red berries of what would become known as the coffee plant, leading to its discovery.

Coffee production in Ethiopia, or Abyssinia as it was known historically, dates back dozens of centuries, and Ethiopia has become Africa's top coffee producer and the world's fifth largest. It is, therefore, not surprising that Ethiopians are coffee lovers, and an elaborate coffee ceremony is a core cultural custom in the country. The ceremony holds significant cultural importance in Ethiopia—where coffee must be the first thing served to guests as a gesture of respect.

While the origins of the coffee plant can be traced back to Ethiopia, the process of preparing roasted coffee beans as a drink is said to have begun on the other side of the narrow Bab Al Mandab Strait, in mid-15th century Yemen, where Sufi monks drank the aromatic brew to keep themselves awake during late-night meditations.[1]

The Arabic word for coffee, *qahwa*, translates from ancient Arabic as "brew." This was an evolution of the Arabic word *qaha*, which refers to a lack of hunger, given the brew had a reputation for provoking a satisfying feeling of fullness.[2]

Pilgrims and traders began transporting Yemeni coffee into other territories, such as Najd and the Hijaz (in present-day Saudi Arabia), resulting in its eventual arrival in Egypt from the Yemeni port of Mokha, the earliest and most famous entrepôt for coffee in the world. Consequently, numerous coffeehouses began to spring up around Makkah, Al Madinah, Jeddah, Cairo and other major cities. These coffeehouses quickly became places where men (and yes, it was only men) would meet and talk, relax and play games such as backgammon and chess. And this is how the first-ever cafés were born. However, I doubt any of those original coffee houses sold chocolate brownies or had free Wi-Fi! After all, who needs free Wi-Fi when you can play chess?

Ban in Makkah

In 1511, Khair Beg Al Mi'mar, the Mamluk governor of Makkah, declared a ban on coffee after his advisors reported that it was a dangerous drug that could provoke radical thinking. They told him coffee was as dangerous an intoxicant as alcohol, which is prohibited by the Qur'an. Consequently, he ordered all coffee to be taken from coffee vendors and burned in the streets. Unfortunately for Khair Beg, the people of Makkah had already embraced coffee, and the official decree from Cairo only disapproved of public gatherings to consume coffee, falling short of an outright ban. So, just one year later, Khair Beg was removed from office and coffee consumption continued unabated. Subsequent jurists in Makkah would decry what they believed to be "sinful" behavior in the holy city's coffee houses but did not renew their calls to ban the popular beverage.[3]

Ottoman Empire

Although coffee spread throughout the Ottoman Empire from the Arabian Peninsula, Arabic coffee and its Turkish counterpart remained quite distinct. While Turkish coffee spread across and beyond the Ottoman Empire, Arabic coffee remained localized in the Arabian Peninsula and its periphery, taking root among both the Bedouin and sedentary Arab communities between the Arabian Gulf and the Red Sea. It became a daily ritual, weaving itself into the diverse fabric of Arab culture.

The understated traditions of Arabic coffee were in stark contrast to the first coffee shops that opened in Istanbul in the middle of the 16th century. As coffee became more popular, its reach expanded to Europe through two routes: by land across the Ottoman Empire and by sea via traders visiting the original coffee port of Mokha.[4]

However, there was a short period in Turkey during the 17th century when the Ottomans could have halted the distribution of coffee. In 1633, the Ottoman Sultan Murad IV (1623-1640) was concerned that conspiracists against his rule were using coffee houses for their gatherings and so perceived as hotbeds for bad behavior. So, he banned public coffee drinking. Although Ibrahim, his successor, reversed the ban, some Islamic scholars remained concerned that the "jolt" of energy coffee delivered could distract believers from their devotional duties. It didn't help the coffee drinkers' cause that the word *qahwa* was also used as an alternative word for wine in Arabic at this time.

While this was a short-lived 17th century theological discussion,[5] it echoed similar debates in Europe with evocations to Pope Clement VIII, whose papacy (1592-1605) resisted the petitions to cast coffee as "the devil's brew." There is a story that the Pope blessed each cup of coffee he drank, but this is likely apocryphal.[6] In 1675, the English monarch King Charles II issued a proclamation to suppress coffee houses and, by extension, the free flow of new ideas, which were an inseparable feature of 17th century English coffee houses.[7] As the proclamation proved unpopular and was ultimately unenforceable, King Charles withdrew the ban just days before it was to come into effect.

The Ottoman-propelled global spread of coffee gathered speed. But in the Arabian Peninsula—both within and beyond the Ottoman sphere of influence—Arabic coffee was prepared as it always had been, without regard to the whims of sultans, popes or kings. Yemen, Oman and the interior of Arabia retained a distinctive Arabic coffee culture, even though coffee beans were now being exported far and wide by English and Dutch commodity traders.

The English and Dutch East India Companies had become the primary global trade operators and exported their large cargoes across the globe. Arguably, this was the beginning of the global availability and mass production of coffee. For many, this international trade distorted coffee's history, creating confusion about where it first originated. Adding to the confusion, production declined significantly in Yemen due to cheap imports and other crops displacing coffee. Indeed, today, there are no top coffee producers among Arab countries, which is unfortunate considering the importance of the arabica bean in creating modern-day coffee. That said, there are efforts underway to revive Yemen's historical coffee industry as well as initiatives to commercially produce coffee in southern Saudi Arabia.

The Middle East has a rich abundance of coffee varieties that have been carefully married with delicate and exquisite spices. Cinnamon, cardamom, saffron and ginger were the traditional spices used in Arabic coffee long before the advent of chemical flavoring. Thanks to the health-boosting compounds in these spices and their holistic benefits, there is a growing interest in Arabic coffee in the Arabian Peninsula and beyond.

Coffee is like ground amber
Black like a lover's eyes
Wafting like a sharp fragrant musk
I likened it to the taste of nectar
Bringing friends together
And binding friendship with a companion
May I not be spared its mixing in my palate.

- Mawla bin Shahin Al Shami

القهوة كالعَنبَر السَّحيق
سَوداء مثلَ مُقْلَة المعشُوق
أتَتْ كَمسك فائح فتيق
شبَّهتُهَا في الطَّعم كَالرَّحيق
تُدني الصَّديقَ من هوى الصَّديق
وتَربطُ الوَدَّ مع الرَّفيق
فلاَ عُدمتُ مَزجَها بريقيي

– المولى بن شاهين الشامي

2. Ingredients

Key Ingredients and Their Health Benefits

Coffee is an intricate mixture of more than a thousand disparate elements. The beauty of fresh Arabic coffee lies not only in its delicious and fragrant flavor, but also in the multitude of health benefits that come with it. Here are some of the key ingredients of Arabic coffee and their primary benefits.

Arabica Coffee Beans

Handpicked with care, each Arabica bean is unique and exudes a distinctive flavor unmatched by any other coffee. The main health benefits associated with Arabica coffee include:

- ◐ *Antioxidant properties.* Arabica beans contain high levels of potent antioxidant compounds that reduce the risk of some types of cancer.[8]

- ◐ *Increased energy levels.* As a natural source of caffeine, which is a central nervous system stimulant, coffee is the perfect drink for improving energy levels. Drinking coffee makes your body and mind more alert, providing the ideal energy boost to maintain an active or busy lifestyle. This makes it a popular beverage during the holy month of Ramadan. When consumed before or after a day of fasting, it gives the body a much-needed energy boost while helping maintain stamina during the day.

- *Reduced risk of some diseases.* According to some studies, regular caffeine consumption can help reduce the risk of developing chronic conditions like Alzheimer's, Parkinson's and type 2 diabetes.[9]

- *Reduced risk of early death.* In one study that followed the health of over 200,000 participants during a 30-year period, those who drank three to five 250ml cups of coffee a day were 15 percent less likely to die early from all causes.[10]

- *Weight loss benefits.* Coffee (when not containing sugar-rich syrups and whipped cream!) is free of calories, meaning you can drink it as much as you like and not worry about weight gain!

Signature Spices and Sides

In the Middle East, something a little extra is added to Arabic coffee blends to make them extraordinary. Coffee is as much about smell as it is about taste. Here are some of the most popular spices and ingredients that can be added to coffee to create countless varieties of incomparable signature flavors and aromas. Health benefits are often ascribed to spices. Cardamom, cloves, cinnamon and ginger have antioxidant properties that can variously decrease blood pressure, reduce inflammation and protect cells from damage.

Cardamom

When infused with cardamom, Arabic coffee takes on a whole new personality and flavor. One of the most complex and tantalizing spices, cardamom has been used since 3,000 BCE, and its sweet and spicy flavors have been enhancing coffee since its advent. What's more, aside from the antioxidant properties, these precious green seeds offer a series of health benefits, which include:

- *Improved digestion.* For centuries, cardamom has aided digestion, and studies have found it can help with gastric ulcers, reducing them in size by a remarkable 50 percent.[11]

- *Weight loss benefits.* According to research, regularly consuming cardamom is associated with a reduction in waist size. When combined with black coffee, cardamom acts as an appetite suppressant and an energy booster that can aid fat loss when used in conjunction with exercise and a healthy diet.

Cloves

Cloves are an intense spice with a distinctive, bold flavor. These exotic and aromatic flower buds provide a delicious accompaniment to Arabic coffee and have a host of additional nutritional and health benefits, such as:

- *Antimicrobial effects.* Cloves contain molecules that have potent antibacterial properties and promote better gut health, helping the body fight infections. They can even improve oral hygiene.

- *Reduced risk of disease.* Beneficial molecules such as eugenol, contained in cloves, can help improve liver function and prevent diseases such as diabetes.

Cinnamon

When it comes to spices, you can't find a more powerful and unmistakable flavor than cinnamon. Perfect with a hot cup of fine Arabic coffee, this fragrant inner tree bark provides a range of beneficial effects for your body, including:

- *Lowered blood sugar.* In individuals with type 2 diabetes, cinnamon has been shown to help to reduce blood glucose levels.[12]

- *Weight loss benefits.* Cinnamon works as an appetite suppressant on its own and in combination with black coffee beans.

Ginger

With its potent and piquant flavor, ginger is an ancient root that may be an acquired taste for some, but it works wonderfully with coffee. Furthermore, ginger has:

- *Anti-nausea properties.* For centuries, ginger has been used to relieve the symptoms of numerous conditions, ranging from pregnancy sickness to vertigo.

- *Antimicrobial properties.* What's more, ginger is also the perfect spice for alleviating cold and flu symptoms. When consumed in a hot drink, it acts as a powerful natural remedy, particularly when combined with honey and lemon.

However, when adding ginger to Arabic coffee, it is important to keep in mind that when consumed in excess, it can also have side effects, such as heartburn and abdominal discomfort.

Saffron

Saffron is an exceptional spice of exquisite delicacy that is a favorite in the Middle East for its distinctive flavor. Derived from the stigma of crocus flowers, it's also the world's most expensive spice, growing only in select regions of the world, with 500g costing anywhere between $600 and $10,000. It pairs beautifully with Arabic coffee, and has numerous health benefits:

- *Relaxation effects.* Saffron can relieve sleep problems, anxiety, depression, and even bipolar disorder.[13]

- *Relief of premenstrual syndrome (PMS) symptoms.* Saffron can also help reduce symptoms associated with PMS, including headaches, abdominal pain, irritability and stress.

Rosewater

Made by distilling rose petals with steam, rosewater is mild and fragrant and pairs delightfully with authentic Arabic coffee, with just a few small drops bringing it to life. In addition to giving your coffee an elegant taste, rosewater also offers important benefits:

- *Skin health benefits.* Rosewater reduces skin irritation due to its anti-inflammatory properties and can be used as a natural supplement for maintaining healthy skin and easing various skin conditions.

- ⟳ *Sore throat treatment.* For centuries, rosewater has helped soothe sore throats, and adding just a few drops to your coffee can alleviate mild throat discomfort.

- ⟳ *Antibacterial properties.* Rosewater is thought to promote the healing of cuts, burns and scars.

The spices and other additives listed above are just some of the key ingredients that can be combined with a beautiful cup of traditional Arabic coffee. With hundreds of potential options to choose from, you will never run out of new coffee flavors, while enjoying the health benefits of Arabic coffee.

Additional Ingredients

Coffee is a form of art, and the ingredients you can use are endless. While writing this book, I discovered hundreds of unique herbs, spices and fruits that families use in Arabic coffee, such as raisins, lemongrass, sesame seeds, nutmeg, thyme, fennel, bay leaf, cocoa powder, turmeric and even black pepper. Here are some of my favorite ingredients that can spice up Arabic coffee.

Orange Blossom Water

As an alternative to rosewater, orange blossom water can be added to coffee in the same measure. The obvious difference between these two ingredients is their taste. With tangy hints of citrus, orange blossom water is commonly found in Morocco, Egypt and Jordan, but it is also available across the Middle East. It is, like the spices used in the coffee, rich in antioxidants and vitamins C and B, it makes a nourishing and delicious addition to your cup of coffee.

Chili Flakes

As you might expect, chili flakes add a hot and spicy punch to coffee. You can stir a few—or a lot—into your cup, but as with any recipe that includes chili, it is a good idea to start with a small amount and increase it gradually to achieve the perfect level of spiciness. I recommend adding chili flakes together with cinnamon to your coffee on cold winter evenings.

Frankincense Gum and Mastic Gum

Frankincense and mastic gums are types of natural tree resins. Although both are widely used in foods in Greece, Turkey and the Middle East, they may seem out of the ordinary to standard coffee drinkers since they are quite rare outside of Yemen and southern Oman. According to studies, chewing frankincense and mastic gums can help prevent cavities and improve oral health. Moreover, they also provide a unique, sweet flavor when paired with coffee. Experimenting with these ingredients is worth a try if you manage to find them. We recommend adding one or two small pieces of the gum to 0.5 liter of boiling coffee and allowing them to dissolve.

Fresh Vanilla Pods

Nothing is more delicious than the aroma of fresh vanilla, and adding this fragrant flavor to your coffee during the boiling process will give your drink a distinctive sweetness. Leaving the vanilla pod uncut is important to prevent the vanilla beans from spreading throughout the coffee, resulting in an overpowering flavor. Keeping the pod uncut will release just enough vanilla flavor to make your coffee pleasantly sweet and easy to drink. Fresh vanilla pods are widely available in shops and markets.

When there is smoke but no coffee, it is like a shepherd with no wool.

- Arabic proverb

دخان بلا قهوة كراعٍ بلا فروة.

– قول شعبي

3. Roasting and Grinding

Roasting

Today, most Arab families buy roasted and ground coffee at supermarkets. However, making coffee from scratch using traditional methods and an open fire remains a popular practice in rural villages, especially among Bedouin tribes. Historically, Bedouins brewed their coffee over a simple fireplace dug into the ground. In sedentary and urban communities, a clay pit with a stove constructed of pebbles and stone plates known as a *kuwar* was used.

The perfect cup of Arabic coffee begins with the finest quality beans—selecting the right beans is the most important part of the process. The right preparation of the beans will bring out their flavor, but there is little you can do during the preparation process to disguise the taste of poor-quality beans.

Coffee beans increase in size when roasted while losing one-fifth of their weight. So, if you're roasting the beans yourself and want to end up with a kilogram of beans, you will need to start with one and a quarter kilograms of unroasted coffee beans.

You can use specialized countertop roasters for this process, but if you don't have a roaster, it's possible to use a heavy frying pan at a temperature over 200 degrees Celsius (392 degrees Fahrenheit). This requires some physical effort, though, as you need to keep rocking the pan, keeping it at a 20-degree angle while stirring the beans constantly to keep them from burning.

Many coffee enthusiasts know that roasting your own beans is worth the time and effort to achieve unique freshness and flavor. After all, coffee is most flavorful during the week after it is roasted. And, of course, you also get to choose between light, medium or dark roasts. The traditional way of roasting coffee beans uses a *mihmaas* (a spoon for stirring the beans) and a *tawa* (a wide circular pan for roasting them). The long handle enables the person doing

Very Light

Saudi Arabia, Bahrain

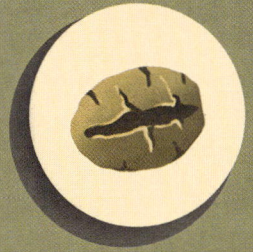

Light

Kuwait, Qatar, United Arab Emirates

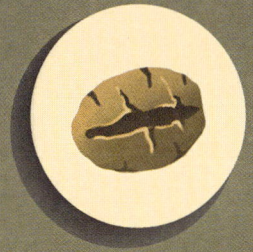

Medium

Oman, Yemen, Egypt

Dark

Lebanon, Syria, Jordan

the roasting to keep a safe distance from the fire while constantly stirring the beans.

As the beans are stirred and roasted, they change color from yellow to orange, and then to brown. The longer they roast, the darker they become. Please keep in mind that a lighter roast corresponds to a more caffeine-rich coffee. Many people who try Arabic coffee for the first time don't expect it to have a lot of caffeine because it has a light color and doesn't taste as strong as espresso. However, even a small cup containing less than 50ml of Arabic coffee has the same amount of caffeine as a medium cup of Americano. The secret to a good coffee recipe is a light-to-medium roast. This will bring out the flavor of the beans without overpowering their taste. If you prefer a darker roast, you can let the beans continue to roast until they reach a shade of darker brown. But take care not to over-roast the beans, as doing so will destroy their flavor.

The constant stirring of the beans as they roast ensures you achieve the essential even color. It is possible to roast spices together with coffee beans to impart their flavors during the roasting process. As we covered in chapter two, you might include cinnamon, cardamom or cloves in the roast to make traditional Arabic coffee. If you decide to roast your own beans, you can try one during the roasting process to test the flavor—they're perfectly edible. However, before you do so, let the beans cool. We recommend transferring hot beans to a wooden container. Roasted beans should be stored in the container for a few days to eliminate the carbon dioxide that builds up inside them during roasting. The wood will preserve their taste.

The Arab world has diverse coffee roasting trends and customs. Typically, traditional Arabic coffee is roasted differently from specialty coffee, while each region has its own unique roasting style and brewing recipes. For instance, the light roasting method is prevalent in Saudi Arabia, and involves roasting the beans right before they begin to crack. Medium-light and medium roasts are more prevalent in Oman and Yemen, and dark roasts are usually preferred in Lebanon, Syria and Iraq. In addition, many Gulf countries incorporate fragrant spices such as cardamom and saffron during the roasting process.

Grinding

There is an art to grinding the beans as evenly as possible. If you want to create a delicious cup of coffee, there are two factors to consider: grind size and consistency. Traditionally, coffee was ground using a pestle and mortar, a tool that dates back to Ancient Egypt, but it can be difficult to achieve a consistent grind using this method. Fortunately, many types of coffee grinders are available on the market these days, including manual and electric ones. There are two main categories of coffee grinders: burr and blade.

A burr grinder (which can be either electric or manual) uses two oscillating "burrs" to grind coffee beans and is a good choice for making ground coffee a consistent size. In contrast, blade coffee grinders use a spinning blade to cut coffee beans. While blade grinders are typically cheaper than burr grinders, they are not always the best choice for producing a consistent grind.

It is important to avoid grinding the beans into a powder, as they need to be coarse enough to be caught by a filter. Arabic coffee should be totally clear. Of course, Bedouins didn't have filters as we know them; they used palm fibers and coconut shells as natural filters.

Nobody comes to the person with no dallah.

- Emirati proverb

اللي ما عنده دله ما حد يندله.

– قول إماراتي

4. Dallah and Finjan

If you're looking to replicate the classic methods of coffee making, it's a good idea to use the traditional Arabic coffee pot, known as a *dallah*, and traditional coffee cups, *finajin* (sing. *finjan*). Let me tell you more about them.

Dallah

Nomadic and sedentary Arab communities have made delicious Arabic coffee in *dallahs* for centuries. Typically, the *dallah* is used to prepare coffee for guests and represents both generosity and wealth. Even today, the *dallah* is a symbol of status and is prized by antique collectors. As a quintessential symbol of Arab culture, the *dallah* is given as a gift on special occasions, such as weddings, births and, more recently, milestone birthdays.

The pots themselves have a bulbous shape and are made of metals such as steel, silver and even gold. Many *dallahs* featured rich ornamentation and were engraved with geometric patterns, plants or Arabic calligraphy, sometimes featuring gemstones. Some craftsmen included the names of the rulers of the region on their creations, so just by examining the design of a *dallah*, experts can often determine its geographical origins.

One of the oldest *dallahs*, dating back to the 17th century, is on display in the Dubai Coffee Museum.[14] Arabic coffee is so central to the culture of the region that a *dallah* is even featured on the back of the one-dirham coin in the United Arab Emirates and is the inspiration for prominent monuments on the corniche of Qatar's capital, Doha, and Abu Dhabi's famous Etihad Square.

If you're worried the *dallah* lacks the convenient features of contemporary coffee pots, then you can rest easy. Thermal and automatic *dallahs* are also available to keep your coffee warm and make the coffee-brewing process easier. These "smart pots" measure water temperature and indicate when it is time to add coffee and spices. They also keep your coffee warm for two to three hours after you prepare it.

Finjan

Arabic coffee is served in a small coffee cup without handles, called a *finjan*, and it is considered impolite to fill it by more than half. The word *finjan* is thought to derive from the word *filj* of a proto-Arabic dialect. *Filj* referred to a vessel for measurement, which may explain the absence of handles on modern-day *finjan*s. Today, the word takes on various iterations in the Arab world, with regions of Saudi Arabia calling it *finjal* and Egyptians pronouncing it *fingan*.[15] Greek and Turkish speakers use words derived from the same stem to describe the small cups (with handles) that are used to drink Greek and Turkish coffee.

Coffee's popularity throughout the Islamic world has led to an increase in the production and propagation of *finjan*s. Travelers to the Middle East often would bring these unique coffee cups home from their journeys, while Arab families imported Chinese and Japanese porcelain (small and handleless), as well as beautiful handcrafted Iranian cups decorated with geometric, floral and Islamic motifs. In the next section, we will discuss making coffee using a *dallah* and **finjan**, as well as the traditional ceremony of coffee making.[16]

The first cup is for the maker; the second is for the guest; the third is for pleasure, and the fourth one is for the sword.

- Arabic proverb

الفنجان الأول للهيف والثاني للضيف والثالث للكيف والرابع للسيف.

– قول شعبي

5. Rituals

The Arabic coffee ceremony is about more than just coffee—it is a deeply social experience that unites friends, family and even strangers. The ceremony is an opportunity to honor one another by taking time to simply be together, sharing a delicious drink and a warm experience.

Coffee is an unspoken language across many Arab regions and has maintained its significance for centuries. In 2015, UNESCO inscribed the Arabic coffee ritual in Oman, Saudi Arabia, Qatar and the UAE on the Representative List of the Intangible Cultural Heritage of Humanity, underscoring its tremendous value to these Arab countries.[17]

Traditions and Arabic Coffee

Coffee can be served across a variety of settings, including the home and at social gatherings and ceremonies. A string of traditions is attached to the humble cup of coffee and the tools used to make it. Coffee is prominent in many ritualistic social occasions, such as weddings, funerals, traditional ceremonies and special religious holidays, such as the holy month of Ramadan and Eid.

As a traditional wedding custom in certain regions, if a guest wished to request something from the host, they would leave their coffee untouched. The host would ask the guest to drink their coffee to indicate his approval of the request. At this point, the guest would need to drink the coffee without asking for water afterwards, as that would be a sign of disrespect, indicating that they want to get rid of the coffee flavor. Even today, this ritual is still followed in some regions.

Historically, coffee was an important symbol at funerals. Bedouins poured coffee onto the ground and turned their *dallah* upside down

as a sign of mourning the dead. You can think of this tradition as analogous to flags being lowered. Indeed, this highlights the central role of Arabic coffee in ceremonies and social customs.

Serving Rituals and Companionship

The coffee ritual was traditionally undertaken by the male hosts, who performed the ceremony in front of their guests, roasting the beans before grinding and brewing them. The entire process, from roasting to serving, took approximately an hour, and a younger member of the family typically carried out the serving. The host tasted the coffee first to ensure it was of good quality, and subsequently offered it to the guests.

As is often still the case today, the serving was conducted from right to left, starting with the most respected member of the family or the guest of honor. The server held the cups in their right hand and the pot in their left. The amount of coffee poured did not exceed one-third of the cup. If the amount poured was greater than half of the cup, it was said to be a sign the guest was not welcome.

As an act of coffee protocol, the guest can let their host know they do not want any more coffee by shaking their cup to indicate they have had enough; otherwise, the host is likely to continue pouring.

The etiquette surrounding the drinking of coffee is also an essential part of the ceremony. The coffee is not gulped as one might with an espresso. It is sipped with contemplation, honoring the ritual of preparation. Arabic coffee is meant to be enjoyed slowly and mindfully; on average, it takes three to five sips to finish one *finjan*. Drinking the entire cup of coffee in one sip is considered impolite.

Arabic Coffee and Mindfulness

Unlike other regular coffee habits, the Arabic coffee ceremony is not practiced "on the go". Historically, the entire process, from roasting coffee beans to grinding and serving cups of coffee, was performed by the host in front of their guests. This process was never rushed and was, and still is, a great tool to ground and center yourself.

In my experience, enjoying Arabic coffee and practicing mindfulness are almost inseparable. As mentioned earlier, Sufi monks shared a similar belief. Centuries ago, when the coffee culture was being spread across the Arabian Peninsula, they used coffee to stay awake during nighttime meditations, as it boosted their energy levels and helped them focus.

In today's hectic world, Arabic coffee offers an opportunity to take a step back, appreciate life and spend quality time with friends and family. Furthermore, it can help us immerse ourselves in a captivating experience that transcends continents and generations.

The greatest thing about a perfectly-timed cup of coffee is that you find it in your hand the moment you crave it. One of the most elegant moments of life is when a small luxury turns into a necessity.

- Mourid Barghouti, Palestinian Poet

أعظم ما في القهوة التَّوْقيت! أن تجدَها في يدك فورَ تتمنّاها. فمن أجملِ أناقات العَيشِ تلكَ اللَّحظةُ التي يتحوَّلُ فيها ترفٌ صغيرٌ إلى ضَرُورة.

– الشاعر الفلسطيني مريد البرغوثي

6. Facts
to Take Away

Ten Interesting facts about coffee that you may not know

Coffee has a rich history, but much of it remains largely unknown. Here are ten facts about coffee we bet you didn't know:

1. The English word "coffee" comes from the Turkish word *kahve*, which, as discussed earlier, owes its origins to the Arabic word *qahwa*, translated as "brew."

2. In 16th century Istanbul, failure to provide your wife with enough coffee was grounds for divorce![18]

3. Coffee beans come from a fruit. Coffee beans are the pit of coffee cherries, which grow on a bush and are classified as fruit precisely because they have this pit.

4. The most popular drink in Yemen—the motherland of coffee—is not coffee. It is, in fact, *qishr* (also spelled *qeshr*, or *cascara* in Latin America), which is made from the dried (but not roasted) husks removed from coffee cherries during production. The husks are then brewed to make tea.[19]

5. Drinking coffee was once punishable by death. During the 17th century in the Ottoman Empire, Sultan Murad IV believed drinking coffee negatively altered drinkers' minds, so it was considered a narcotic.[20]

6. The first clear historical evidence of grinding beans and brewing them into a cup of coffee dates back to 15th century Yemen.[21]

7. The drink mocha, which consists of a mixture of hot chocolate and espresso, comes from the port of Mokha in Yemen, the first place from which coffee was exported.

8. A recent study found that people who have a penchant for caffeine also have a strong preference for the smell and taste of coffee and dark chocolate.[22]

9. In the 1730s, Johan Sebastian Bach, one of the most successful music composers in history, wrote a comic mini-opera called the *Coffee Cantata* about a woman who was addicted to coffee. It includes the following lyric: "If I couldn't, three times a day, be allowed to drink my little cup of coffee, in my anguish I would turn into a shriveled-up roast goat." It seems coffee addiction is not a modern phenomenon!

10. Historically, Arabs used *finjan*s to measure out the correct amount of coffee during the preparation process. It is still practiced to this day by some families.[23]

The first cup is for my head, the second is for my strength and courage and the third is for my headache.

  - Arabic proverb

الفنجان الأوّل لراسي والثّاني لبأسي والثالث لعُماسي .

– قول شعبي

7. Tips and Tricks

Over the years of my coffee journey, I have gathered some clever tips and tricks for creating the optimal aromatic profile and taste for my Arabic coffee. I'm happy to share them here to help you create your best cup yet.

1. Avoid using metal utensils when stirring coffee and mixing in spices. This is because the presence of metal can negatively impact the coffee's taste. Instead, you can use a cinnamon stick or a wooden spoon to stir the coffee.

2. If you plan to use saffron to spice your coffee, it is best to add it at the beginning of the coffee brewing process – before the water begins to boil. When added at the end of the brewing process, saffron may not properly dissolve, and can be overpowered by coffee beans.

3. After brewing your coffee, avoid serving it immediately. Instead, let it settle for five to ten minutes to develop its optimal flavor. You may want to keep it in a special kettle to keep it warm, but wait to serve it, as the taste will be completely different if drunk too soon.

4. When selecting roasted coffee beans, I recommend using light or medium roast, since dark roasts tend to overpower the spices.

5. When grinding coffee beans, it is best to avoid a fine grind. This is because Arabic coffee should be textured – the coarser the grind, the better the coffee flavor.

Coffee is our gold. Wherever it is served, one enjoys the company of the noblest and most generous of men.

- Arabic proverb

القهوة هي ذهبنا. أينما يَتِمُّ تقديمها، يستمتعُ المرءُ بصُحبةِ أنبلِ الرِّجالِ و أكرِمِهِم .

– قول شعبي

8. Recipes

The Original Qahwa

cardamom

saffron

cinnamon

rose water

specialty arabica coffee beans

Brewing the Original Qahwa is an experience to savor. Here is our simple step-by-step method to help you build the aroma and intensify the flavors to create an amazing cup of coffee.

INGREDIENTS

400ml filtered water

2 Tbsp of freshly ground arabica coffee

½ Tbsp of ground cardamom

5 to 8 threads of saffron

A pinch of cinnamon

1 Tbsp of distilled rose water

Dates or halwa (optional; to be served with coffee)

MATERIALS

Wooden spoon or cinnamon stick to stir the liquid

Measuring spoon

Coffee pot or *dallah*

Traditional Arabic coffee cups (*finjans*)

METHOD

1. Gently warm the water in the pot or *dallah* over a low heat and add the saffron so it floats on the surface.

2. When the water starts to bubble gently, add the ground coffee and ground cardamom.

3. Stir the liquid gently using a wooden spoon until the coffee begins to boil and release its spiced aroma.

4. Once the coffee comes to a rolling boil, remove it from the heat and let it rest for a moment.

5. Return the pot to low heat for five more minutes.

6. Add cinnamon and keep the pot on low heat for an additional two to three minutes.

7. Remove the pot from the heat, add rose water and allow the liquid to stand for five minutes to calm its heat and settle before serving. Arabic coffee should never be so hot as to burn your tongue or require you to blow across its surface to cool it down.

8. Serve the coffee in traditional Arabic coffee cups with fresh dates or halwa for an authentic Arab experience.

Intense Qahwa

cinnamon   cardamom   saffron

specialty arabica
coffee beans

There are moments when life calls for an espresso. Here is an ancient recipe to create an espresso with the rich and powerful taste of traditional Arabic coffee. You simply must try this Intense *Qahwa*! Brewed to perfection, it can be the perfect start to your morning. It is also an ideal alternative base for cappuccino, latte or flat white.

INGREDIENTS

200ml filtered water

2 Tbsp of freshly ground arabica coffee

⅓ Tbsp of ground cardamom

5 to 8 threads of saffron

A pinch of cinnamon

Dates or halwa (optional; to be served with coffee)

MATERIALS

Wooden spoon or cinnamon stick to stir the liquid

Pot or *dallah*

Traditional Arabic coffee cups (*finjan*s)

METHOD

1. Warm the water in the pot and add the saffron so it floats on the surface.

2. When the water starts to boil, add the ground coffee and ground cardamom.

3. Stir the liquid gently using the wooden spoon until the coffee begins to boil.

4. Remove the coffee pot from the heat and let it rest briefly.

5. Return the deep, dark, aromatic coffee to low heat for five more minutes.

6. Add the cinnamon and keep the pot on low heat for two to three more minutes as the simmering coffee absorbs the cinnamon.

7. Remove the pot from the heat and allow the rich liquid to stand still for five minutes to cool and settle before serving.

8. Serve in traditional Arabic coffee cups with fresh dates or halwa for an authentic Arab experience.

Arabic Latte

Steamed
Milk

Intense
Qahwa

Europeans have been combining coffee with milk since the middle of the 17th century. Originating in Italy, the latte has become an essential part of the daily morning routine for many people across the globe. Some Italians frown upon adding milk to coffee after breakfast. However, here in the Middle East, we are not so strict, and in countries like Syria and Palestine, people have even invented their own special variations of the humble latte. We may be biased, but we believe our Arabic lattes can't be beaten! The Arabic latte is rich and creamy with a hint of our signature spices, making it a delight for the senses. What more could you want? Just make sure you have a whisk or a milk frother on hand to froth your milk for this delicious recipe!

INGREDIENTS

50ml shot of Intense Qahwa (see recipe above)

200ml milk (whole milk works best, but you can also use almond or coconut milk for this recipe)

A few threads of saffron (for decoration)

MATERIALS

Milk frother or whisk

Barista spoon

Mug

METHOD

1. Prepare your Intense Qahwa shot and pour 50ml of it into your mug of choice. This recipe calls for a mug you can hold with both hands, so right before you take your first sip, you can smell the aroma of the coffee's fragrant spice.

2. Heat your milk until it's very hot, but not quite boiling.

3. Froth your milk until it is thick, creamy and devoid of bubbles.

4. Fold the frothed milk onto the coffee using your barista spoon to hold back the foam.

5. Spoon the remaining foam on top of the coffee.

6. Place two or three saffron threads on the very top of the milk foam to add a colorful flourish to your Arabic Latte.

Arabic Macchiato

Milk Foam

Intense
Qahwa

The intensity of Arabic coffee can be overwhelming for some, especially if you are a beginner and are just trying it for the first time. Macchiato is the perfect way to ease your introduction to the authentic taste of Arabic coffee. Using slightly foamed milk will take the edge off the intense coffee flavor and give you a milder result. The foam should only take up ⅓ of the cup or less. In this recipe, the Arabic coffee remains the star, but its intensity is toned down a bit.

INGREDIENTS

60ml of Intense Qahwa (see recipe above)

30ml of milk (whole milk works best)

MATERIALS

Espresso cup

Milk frother or whisk

Barista spoon

METHOD

1. Prepare your Intense Qahwa shot and pour 60ml of it into your cup.

2. Heat the milk until it is very hot, but not quite boiling.

3. Froth the milk until it produces a thick, creamy froth, while ensuring there are no bubbles.

4. Scoop out a dollop of foam and add it to the top of your Qahwa Espresso.

5. Decorate your latte by placing a few saffron threads on the foamed milk.

Iced Qahwa

specialty arabica
coffee beans

ginger syrup

Many parts of the Middle East can get very hot during the summer months. Nothing beats the heat like a tasty and refreshing Iced Qahwa. You may be tempted to drink ten of these, although we do not recommend consuming that much caffeine!

INGREDIENTS

400ml of the Original Qahwa (see recipe above)

Ice cubes

1 tsp of organic, sugar-free ginger syrup (or any other flavor of your choice)

MATERIALS

200ml glass

METHOD

1. Prepare the Original Qahwa (using the above recipe), pour it into a pot and place it in the refrigerator to chill.

2. Add one teaspoon of organic, sugar-free ginger syrup to the coffee and stir the liquid using a wooden spoon or cinnamon stick.

3. Pour 100ml of the coffee mixture into a glass and add some ice. *Tip: the amount of ice should be equal to the amount of coffee in the glass.

4. Serve immediately.

Arabic Cappuccino

Milk Foam

Steamed Milk

Intense Qahwa

The cappuccino is one of the most famous coffee drinks in the world, and for good reason – it is so delicious! Dating back to 18th century Vienna, it was first created with strong coffee, whipped cream and spices. A shot of arabica brew can bring a cappuccino to life. Those looking for the real Arabic Cappuccino (or "Qahwaccino") experience can add some coconut or almond milk and sprinkle a bit of cinnamon on top. However, you can also try it with a variety of different milk or spice combinations.

INGREDIENTS

60ml of Intense Qahwa (see recipe above)

120ml of milk (whole milk works best)

A few threads of saffron for decoration

MATERIALS NEEDED

Milk frother or whisk

200ml coffee mug

Spoon

METHOD

1. Pour the Intense Qahwa into a mug.

2. Heat the milk (either in the microwave or in a saucepan) until it is very hot, but not quite boiling.

3. Froth the milk until it forms a thick foam (of about 2 to 3cm) and no more bubbles.

4. Once the milk is frothed, pour the milk into the Intense Qahwa while using a spoon to hold back the foam. Then, pour the remaining foam on top.

5. As you fill the cup, move the jug closer to pour the mix into its center.

6. A few threads of saffron transport the cappuccino from Italy to the Arab world.

Intense Qahwa

Vanilla Ice Cream

Affogato Qahwa

Although it is not a drink, this Arab take on a classic Italian dessert is worth a try if you are looking for something a little sweeter than you might be used to. Pairing a scoop of rich and creamy vanilla ice cream with some fresh Arabic coffee is a match made in heaven.

INGREDIENTS

60ml of Intense Qahwa (see recipe above)

1 scoop vanilla ice cream

MATERIALS NEEDED

Glass

Ice cream scoop

METHOD

1. Prepare your Intense Qahwa.

2. Place one scoop of vanilla ice cream into a glass and pour the Intense Qahwa on top of it.

3. Enjoy!

Moka Pot

cardamom   cinnamon   saffron

specialty arabica
coffee beans

If you'd like to try out another classic coffee, then the moka pot is as traditional as it gets. Named after the old Yemeni port of Mokha, where coffee was sold in the 15th century, this coffeepot was invented by Italian engineers, Luigi di Ponti and Alfonso Bialetti, in 1933. They changed coffee history by making it possible to create espresso-like coffee at home. In the Middle East, we put our own spin on coffee brewed in the moka pot by adding some delicious spices to make it even more special. Let's look at how you can use the moka pot to make incredibly delicious Arabic coffee.

INGREDIENTS

200ml filtered water

1 Tbsp of freshly ground arabica coffee

½ tsp of ground cardamom

A pinch of cinnamon

A few threads of saffron

MATERIALS NEEDED
Moka pot (200ml)

Mug

METHOD

1. Fill the bottom chamber of the moka pot with water to the level of the valve.

2. Place the coffee powder trough (also known as the "basket," which holds the ground coffee) into the water base (also known as the "bottom chamber"). If water enters the trough, pour out the excess water and place the trough into the water base again.

3. Loosely fill the trough with a blend of ground coffee and spices while avoiding compacting them.

4. Assemble your moka pot, ensuring the rim is clean, and the pot is held together firmly.

5. Brew the pot on a gas stove. As the water in the bottom chamber starts boiling, the pressure will steadily push a stream of coffee into the upper chamber.

6. Once the coffee finishes spurting out, take the pot off the heat and pour the coffee into cups.

Tip: It is best to clean the moka pot as soon as it is cool enough to handle. Also, remember that a moka pot will not be fully compatible with an electric stove, and since aluminum is a good heat conductor, the pot will overheat quickly. Moreover, if you have an induction stovetop, you will need to use an induction-compatible moka pot.

Spiced Qahwa

cardamom

saffron

cinnamon

chili flakes

specialty arabica coffee beans

If you are looking to add a little heat to cold winter days when the weather calls for a thick sweater and scarf, then look no further than this delicious Spiced Qahwa. It is the perfect coffee for cold autumn and winter mornings, and it also makes a great accompaniment on long walks when kept warm in a thermal flask. Its ingredients are widely available, and the recipe is as easy to make as a regular Arabic Qahwa, but it contains a few added surprises.

INGREDIENTS

400ml filtered water

2 Tbsp of ground arabica coffee

½ Tbsp of ground cardamom

A few threads of saffron

A pinch of cinnamon

A pinch of chili flakes

Dates or halwa (optional; to be served with coffee)

MATERIALS

Wooden spoon

Measuring spoon

Coffee pot or *dallah*

Traditional Arabic coffee cups or a vacuum flask

METHOD

1. Heat the water in the pot and add the saffron.

2. As the water starts to boil, add the ground coffee, ground cardamom and chili flakes.

3. Gently stir the coffee using a wooden spoon until it boils.

4. Once boiled, remove the coffee from the heat and let it rest for a moment.

5. Return the coffee to the heat for five more minutes.

6. Add cinnamon and keep the coffee on low heat for an additional two to three minutes.

7. Remove the pot from the heat and allow the rich, aromatic liquid to infuse for five more minutes, allowing it to cool and settle before serving.

8. Serve in traditional Arabic coffee cups with fresh dates or halwa for an authentic Arab experience or bring it along for your walk in a portable mug!

Tip: Pack a few dates or a generous chunk of halwa in a sealed sandwich bag for a cheeky little snack away from home if you plan to take your coffee with you on the go.

cardamom

saffron

specialty arabica
coffee beans

Saudi Qahwa

by Sara Alali

Among all the types of coffee I brew, Arabic coffee is my favorite to prepare, and I like to enjoy it in the company of others. In Saudi Arabia, Arabic coffee is usually at the center of any gathering, whether among friends or family, or at a special event. This is why it is so important for it to be brewed well. If the coffee does not taste good, it can really take the joy out of a gathering.

Saudi coffee, or *qahwa*, is known for its light roasted bean profile compared to the types of roasts used in other parts of the Arab world. Some local variations of the roast profile also exist, with preference often given to darker roasts in the north of Saudi Arabia, and lighter roasts in the regions of the south. The taste profile of Saudi *qahwa* is typically nutty, with hints of peanut. What's more, cardamom and saffron are the staple spices used. To enjoy the perfect cup, it is essential to only use quality ingredients.

INGREDIENTS

45g light roasted arabica coffee beans (I prefer Costa Rican and Yemeni varieties for this recipe)

800ml cold filtered water

5-8 threads of saffron

20g of medium ground cardamom

MATERIALS

Bamboo stirring spoon

1-liter *dallah* for brewing

6 *finjan*s

1-liter serving *dallah*

INSTRUCTIONS

1. Bring the cold water to a boil.

2. Add the freshly ground coffee beans (with the grind the size of caster sugar).

3. Brew the coffee with the saffron for approximately 16 minutes.

4. Add the cardamom, and once it reaches a full, rolling boil, quickly remove the *dallah* from the heat.

5. Leave the grounds to settle for two minutes.

6. Decant the brewed coffee while pouring it through a mesh strainer into the serving *dallah*.

7. Serve the coffee with high-quality dates and enjoy!

Sara Alali

Founder and Co-Owner - THAT Boutique Cafe in Riyadh, Saudi Arabia

Barista trainer and Q-grader

Sensory judge in Qahwa Championship 2019

Host of The MAP IT FORWARD Middle East Podcast World Cezve/ Ibrik Championship Finalist

Turkish Qahwa

by John Leonida

Coffee was more than a little cup of hospitality to my Cypriot immigrant parents. Their coffee encompassed the memories, aromas and flavors of their small village of Kalopanayiotis in the Troodos mountains. Sometimes, it was the top note of a fragrant breakfast of halloumi, tomatoes, cucumber and fresh village bread. It was a reminiscence of the village coffee shop, where the coffee was always served with a cube of Turkish delight (known as *lokumi* in Greek) and a glass of water on the side. I have sipped that coffee in Kalopanayiotis, Athens, Istanbul and Alexandria, a legacy of the Ottoman Empire, which lasted from 1299 to 1922. Turkish coffee is sometimes called Greek coffee and there are versions of it originating from the Baltic states to the Balkans, but Turkish coffee by any other name is still Turkish coffee. Or, at least, this is my personal take on Turkish coffee. Turkish coffee is finely ground and densely packed. The Greek and Egyptian roasts are quite light, while the Turkish and Cypriot roasts are darker. You cannot use espresso coffee—the roast and grind are all wrong.

And, as a final word, one doesn't make Turkish coffee; one cooks it.

85

INGREDIENTS

1 heaping tsp of Turkish coffee (fine ground arabica) per cup

1 Turkish coffee cup of filtered water per cup of coffee

Sugar, depending on how sweet you want your coffee (optional)

½ tsp of ground cardamon or Medina Starlight Blend© per cup (optional)

MATERIALS

A cezve, also known as a *briki* (Greek) or an *ibrik* (Turkish), is a small pot with a long handle and an open neck that is narrower than its base

Turkish coffee cups

METHOD

1. Start by pouring cold water into the cezve (one Turkish coffee cup of water per cup of coffee).

2. Add the Turkish coffee to the cezve and stir.

3. Add the sugar (optional). There are several levels of sweetness of Turkish coffee: plain, without sugar; medium, containing one teaspoon of sugar; and sweet, which requires two teaspoons of sugar. The sugar should be added to the cold coffee slurry before it heats up.

4. To give this Turkish coffee a *qahwa* twist, add the cardamon or the Medina Starlight Blend© to the cezve.

5. Place the cezve on medium heat while continuously stirring the slurry, until a gentle head of foam begins

to rise up the sides of the cezve. As the foam begins to reach the neck of the cezve, it will fold in on itself.

6. Remove the cezve from the heat and allow the foam to subside. Do not allow the coffee to boil or bubble continuously.

7. Gently, knock the base of the cezve on the countertop before returning the pot to the heat.

8. Repeat steps five, six and seven two more times. Do not stir the mix.

9. After the third rising of the coffee, remove the cezve from the heat, knock it on the countertop one more time to settle the coffee grounds and pour the dark liquid through its foam into the cups. Then, divide the coffee foam (known as the *kaimaki* in Greek) equally between the cups you are serving. Turkish coffee served without *kaimaki* is nearly an imprisonable offense! Avoid stirring; the coffee grounds will naturally settle at the bottom of the cup.

10. Serve the coffee with a glass of cold water and a piece of Turkish delight. Alternatively, you can also serve it with breakfast instead of tea.

John Leonida

Economist, Lawyer, Historian, Superyacht journalist, writer of tales and host of the Clyde & Co Superyacht podcast. Indulging in coffee at every possible opportunity

Qahwa Qishr

ginger

cinnamon

sugar

qishr

by Fatma Al-Baiti

In Yemen, no part of the coffee plant gets left behind. *Qishr*, which literally translates to 'shell,' refers to the coffee husks used to make Yemeni Qahwa Qishr, which is typically served as an alternative to coffee. Notably, qishr coffee does not need to be roasted and is lower in caffeine and flavor intensity than traditional coffee. The addition of spices to Yemeni *qishr* is optional – it is perfectly aromatic and flavorful on its own.

I was not familiar with Qahwa Qishr when growing up in Yemen, since my parents did not make it at home, but I discovered it later in life at a colleague's family event. It was light, both in color and flavor. I remember enjoying it so much that I asked for the recipe. I also learned it's a common favorite in northern Yemen and is often served instead of coffee, as it minimizes waste and has less caffeine. I find it amusing that Qahwa Qishr has now become trendy worldwide. If only people knew that Yemenis were unintentionally ahead of the curve!

INGREDIENTS

4 cups of filtered water (250ml/cup)

2 tsp of roughly ground *qishr*

½ tsp of freshly grated or ground ginger (optional)

¼ tsp of ground cinnamon (optional)

Sugar to taste (optional)

MATERIALS

Regular cup or a small mug

Measuring spoon

Regular saucepan (with a pouring spout, if available)

Wooden spoon

Small sieve

METHOD

1. Pour the water into a saucepan and bring it to a boil.

2. Add the ground coffee husks (*qishr*).

3. If you would like to add spices, add the ginger and cinnamon (optional).

4. Gently mix the coffee with a wooden spoon.

5. Once the mix begins to rise in the saucepan (a minute or two later), lower the heat to medium-low and let it brew for another 10 to 15 minutes until the coffee turns golden brown.

6. Remove the saucepan from heat, use a sieve to strain

the husks and pour the *qishr* into a pot or straight into your cups.

Fatma Al-Baiti

Founder of Yemeni brunch pop-up series "Meet me at Fatma's" (London)

Food show host on Nas Aden

Blogger and content creator with a focus on Yemeni cuisine

© Fatma Al-Baiti 2023

Emirati Qahwa

saffron

cardamom

specialty arabica coffee beans

Serves **8-10** people

by Nooran Albannay

Coffee is my passion, and I love the way it connects us with different cultures and memories. My love for coffee dates back to my childhood when my beloved grandmother made *gahwa* – as we pronounce it in the UAE – in the early morning. I still remember its enticing smell filling the house as I was getting ready for school. Every morning, I would greet my grandmother and she would tell me how her *gahwa* had turned out that day and ask me what I'd like to have for lunch when I returned from school. These fond memories have served as a source of inspiration for me.

In UAE, *gahwa* and dates are present in every home as a symbol of hospitality. Help yourself to a cup of this traditional Emirati Qahwa coffee blend made with coffee beans, cardamom and saffron. It represents the true taste of Emirati culture! This recipe has been passed down in my family from my dear grandmother with love, care and joy.

91

INGREDIENTS

80g coarsely ground arabica coffee (we used a 50-50 Brazilian-Sri Lankan blend or Ethiopian varieties)

2 tsp of ground cardamom

1 liter of cold filtered water

A few threads of saffron

*Note: the color of the roasted coffee beans should be brown or light brown (light to medium roast).

MATERIALS

Coffee *dallah* (large enough to hold 1.2-1.5l)

INSTRUCTIONS

1. Slowly bring the cold water to a boil (for about two minutes).

2. Add the freshly ground coffee beans.

3. Stir in two teaspoons of cardamom.

4. Let the mixture boil slowly for an additional 15-20 minutes.

5. Transfer the *gahwa* to the *dallah* and add a few threads of saffron.

6. Let the *gahwa* steep for ten minutes and then serve it in *finjan*s.

Nooran Albannay

Founder and CEO – "Coffee Architecture" in Abu Dhabi, UAE

Owner – Section Coffee Roaster in Abu Dhabi, UAE

Q Arabica Grader since 2017

Authorized Specialty Coffee Trainer since 2021

Meet Medina Coffee Company

Medina Coffee Company is on a mission to connect people to each other and to our planet through the world's original coffee.

Based in Oman and delighting customers all over the world, Medina Coffee Company delivers the world's best Arabic coffee experience to coffee lovers across the globe. At Medina Coffee Company, we have reinvented the traditional Arabic coffee ritual for the modern world. Join us from anywhere and enjoy all the physical, social, and emotional perks of the ancient coffee ceremony!

About Our Coffee

The complex flavor profile of Medina Coffee originates from rare, high-quality, organic arabica beans. Our single-origin beans are grown, harvested and processed using traditional practices that are kind to the Earth, and benefit our coffee farmers by supporting the communities they live in. Medina Coffee doesn't taste like the coffee you usually buy at a grocery store. It has a deep, earthy flavor with a satisfying, lingering finish and also carries hints of exquisite Arabic spices such as cardamom and saffron.

Our extraordinary arabica coffee is certified by the Specialty Coffee Association, a coffee grading organization dedicated to quality, fairness, and sustainability.

Acknowledgments

First and foremost, I would like to express my sincere gratitude to my parents for always believing in me and encouraging me in all my endeavors. My father deserves a special thank you – together, we have tried over 100 coffee recipes and roasted over 50 varieties of arabica coffee beans.

I would also like to thank my mother- and father-in-law for supporting my ideas and helping me implement them.

Thank you to my dear husband, Usama, who doesn't believe in failing, always pushes me forward and agrees to try my new coffee recipes.

I am grateful to Sara Alali for finding the time to contribute to this book and for preserving the Arabic heritage.

If I wore a hat, I would tip it in the direction of the ever-dapper John Leonida for his priceless contribution and efforts, as well as for our non-stop, months-long conversation discussing the history, recipes, rituals and the future of Arabic coffee. And yes, John wears countless hats.

I raise a paintbrush in honor of Olha Rybtsova, an amazing Ukrainian artist who continued to work on my book project despite being forced from her hometown because of the ongoing invasion.

Thank you to my best friend Karima for motivating me to go forward and open a school of Arabic coffee.

I would also like to thank my brother Askar, who has always given me unwavering support and allows me to be myself.

I sincerely appreciate the efforts of Professor Christian Elger, who rescued me and gave me a chance to find my new passion.

Thanks to my wonderful children Razan, Mohammed, and Dania–this book is for you. I want to preserve this invaluable heritage for the younger generations.

Last but not least, I would like to recognize Jill Bobrow, Fatma Makki, Afra Al Said, Sagar Jaitly, Nooran Albannay, Meruyert Shagmanova, Sara Al Aulaqi, Peter Harrigan, Jeff Eamon, Alexandra Lawson, Rachel Hamilton, Dr Hanan Elsayed and the rest of the team at Medina Publishing. And, of course, thanks to everyone who has attended my classes and shared my love of Arabic coffee.

References

[1] Jonathan Morris, *Coffee: A Global History* (London: Reaktion Books, 2019), 23.

[2] Ralph S. Hattox, *Coffee and Coffeehouses: The Origins of a Social Beverage in the Medieval Near East* (Seattle: University of Washington Press, 1988), 11-28.

[3] Ibid., 29-45.

[4] John McHugo, "Coffee and qahwa: How a drink for Arab mystics went global," *BBC News* (April 2013), https://www.bbc.com/news/magazine-22190802 (accessed 18 December 2022).

[5] Daniel W. Brown, *A New Introduction to Islam* (New Jersey: John Wiley & Sons Ltd, 2017), 270-309.

[6] Tom Standage, *A History of the World in 6 Glasses* (New York: Bloomsbury Publishing, 2006).

[7] Keith Suter, "The Rise and Fall of English Coffee Houses," *Contemporary Review* 286 (1669): 107-110.

[8] Rince Alfia Fadri et al., "Phytochemical Screening and Antioxidant Test of Arabika Roasted Coffee Bean Extract (*Coffea arabica* L.) from Agam Regency," *IOP Conf. Series: Earth and Environmental Science* 1097 (2022).

[9] Debbie Lambert, "Drinking coffee may reduce the risk of developing Alzheimer's disease," *Medical News Today* (November 2021), https://www.medicalnewstoday.com/articles/drinking-coffee-may-reduce-the-risk-of-developing-alzheimers-disease

(accessed 18 December 2022); Xiangpeng Ren and Jiang-Fan Chen, "Caffeine and Parkinson's Disease: Multiple Benefits and Emerging Mechanisms," *Frontiers in Neuroscience* 14 (2020); Shilpa N. Bhupathiraju et al., "Changes in coffee intake and subsequent risk of type 2 diabetes: three large cohorts of US men and women," *Diabetologia* (2014).

[10] Harvard T.H. Chan School of Public Health, *Coffee*, https://www.hsph.harvard.edu/nutritionsource/food-features/coffee/ (accessed 18 December 2022).

[11] Jamal A. et al., "Gastroprotective effect of cardamom, Elettaria cardamomum Maton. fruits in rats," *Journal of Ethnopharmacology* 103 no. 2 (2005): 149-153.

[12] S. Kirkham et al., "The potential of cinnamon to reduce blood glucose levels in patients with type 2 diabetes and insulin resistance," *Diabetes, Obesity and Metabolism: A Journal of Pharmacology and Therapeutics* 11 no. 12 (December 2009): 1100-1113.

[13] Mojtaba Shafiee et al., "Saffron in the treatment of depression, anxiety and other mental disorders: Current evidence and potential mechanisms of action," *Journal of Affective Disorders* 227 no. 6 (November 2017): 330-337.

[14] Coffee Museum, *About the Museum*, http://www.coffeemuseum.ae (accessed 18 December 2022).

[15] Ahd Fadhel, "fi yom al qahwa.. hatha asl kalimat Finjan fi al lughat al arabiya" [On Coffee Day.. This is the Origin of the Word Finjan in Arabic], *Al Arabiyah* (1 October 2019), https://www.alarabiya.net/culture-and-art/2019/10/01/في-يوم-القهوة-هذا-أصل-كلمة-فنجان-في- اللغة-العربية (accessed 18 December 2022).

[16] The British Museum, *Life in a cup: coffee culture in the Islamic world*, https://www.britishmuseum.org/sites/default/files/2021-10/Life_in_a_cup_coffee_culture_in_the_Islamic_world_large_print_guide_1021.pdf (accessed 18 December 2022).

[17] UNESCO: Intangible Cultural Heritage, *Arabic coffee, a symbol of generosity*, https://ich.unesco.org/en/RL/%20arabic-coffee-a-symbol-of-generosity-01074 (accessed 18 December 2022).

[18] Ebru Boyar and Kate Fleet, *A Social History of Ottoman Istanbul* (Cambridge: Cambridge University Press, 2010), 270.

[19] James Hoffman, *The World Atlas of Coffee: From Beans to Brewing – Coffee Explored, Explained and Enjoyed* (Ontario: Firefly Books, 2014), 175.

[20] Mark Hay, "In Istanbul, Drinking Coffee in Public Was Once Punishable by Death," *Atlas Obscura* (22 May 2018), https://www.atlasobscura.com/articles/was-coffee-ever-illegal (accessed 18 December 2022).

[21] Hattox, *Coffee and Coffeehouses*, 11-28.

[22] Marilyn C. Cornelis and Rob M. van Dam, "Genetic determinants of liking and intake of coffee and other bitter foods and beverages," *Scientific Reports* 11 no. 1 (2021).

[23] British Museum, *Life in a cup.*